T0132188

Treatment Planning from a Reality Therapy Perspective

Michael H. Fulkerson, LPCC

TREATMENT PLANNING FROM A REALITY THERAPY PERSPECTIVE

iUniverse books may be ordered through booksellers or by contacting:

iUniverse
1663 Liberty Drive
Bloomington, IN 47403
www.iuniverse.com
1-800-Authors (1-800-288-4677)

ISBN: 978-1-4917-4322-5 (sc)
ISBN: 978-1-4917-4323-2 (e)

Library of Congress Control Number: 2014914632

Printed in the United States of America.

iUniverse rev. date: 1/09/2015

Contents

Contents

Preface

With the second edition of the publication, I have changed the name from *Treatment Planning from a Choice Theory Perspective* to *Treatment Planning from a Reality Therapy Perspective.* I have two primary reasons for this title change. First, reality therapy is how it is listed in all the counseling theories textbooks. Calling "reality therapy" by the name "choice theory" is similar to calling "behavior therapy" by the name "stimulus-response theory." None of the other methods of psychotherapy are referred to as just theories. In my opinion, it makes senses to refer to the practice of choice theory in psychotherapy as reality therapy. Second, reality therapy is a title synonymous with Dr. William Glasser and will be his legacy.

In addition to the title change, I have also made some other additions to the book. First, I have expanded chapter 2 by providing a more thorough description of using reality therapy in treatment planning, including a more extensive description of treatment outcome measures. Second, I have added two chapters. Chapter 5 will cover documentation of progress notes, and chapter 7 will compare reality therapy treatment planning with other models of psychotherapy. Finally, I have added page numbers and a table of contents to help make the book more organized and reader friendly.

Acknowledgments

My hope is that this book will be a helpful resource to those wishing to incorporate the method known as reality therapy into treatment planning. Although there have been many books written regarding a variety of topics based on choice theory/reality therapy, the information regarding the application of this approach on the topic of treatment planning has been sparse. My wish is that this book will help fill some of the void.

Thanks to Kim Olver, Bob Wubbolding, Brian Jones, Mary Kay Lamb, and Jim Evans for their suggestions, recommendations, and encouragement. This book is dedicated to the late Dr. William Glasser and Dr. J. Robert Cockrum.

Chapter 1: Introduction

1

Treatment Planning from a Reality Therapy Perspective
Synopsis

Treatment Planning from a Reality Therapy Perspective is designed to be a primer for mental health practitioners desiring to write treatment plans from a reality therapy perspective. This book provides an explanation of how reality therapy treatment planning differs from traditional treatment planning models, which are usually based on the medical model and/ or external control psychology. Examples of how to write treatment goals and objectives that are precise and measurable are illustrated. Treatment plans from a reality therapy perspective have been field-tested by a clinician who has received numerous successful reviews from the Council for the Accreditation of Rehabilitative Facilities (CARF), the Office of the Inspector General (OIG), and several managed care organizations (MCOs).

I.   Introduction

Most treatment planning books are based on the medical model and/or external control psychology approaches, such as behavior modification. Most psychotherapists use the diagnosis as the central guidance mechanism in the development of a treatment plan. Using the diagnosis of the client, the psychotherapist uses a treatment planner to identify goals and objectives associated with the mental illness diagnosis. The expectation is that the diagnosis will provide the clinician with the information to develop an appropriate treatment plan for the client.

Treatment strategies are based on what are often highly questionable diagnoses in which a treatment team of behavioral health professionals is unable to come to an agreement regarding the diagnosis. Furthermore, since these subjective diagnoses are based on treating mental illness, the goals and objectives are often not strength-based and may in fact have little to do with the client's actual presenting problems.

My purpose for developing *Treatment Planning from a Reality Therapy Perspective* was to provide some examples of how to develop treatment plans from more of a public health model rather than from a medical model. The inspiration for this project was Dr. William Glasser's booklet entitled *Defining Mental Health as a Public Health Issue* (2005), where he advocates the necessity of shifting from the medical model to a public health model.

According to the medical model, client diagnoses are viewed as the sources of the problem. The overemphasis on using diagnosing as a basis of treatment planning seems to foster more of an external locus of control with clients. Often these clients will perceive themselves as helpless, eternal victims. In addition to the stigma of receiving dehumanizing labels, such as "bipolar," "schizophrenic," "psychotic," or "ADHD," these clients continually receive discouraging messages from the outside world (including the behavioral health profession) that they are incapable of being successful.

For almost twenty years, I have witnessed clients coming to my office for a first-time appointment with the belief that a mental illness diagnosis was their primary issue. They have appeared to be greatly enlightened when I inform them of how they obtained their diagnosis. Sometimes they are surprised to learn that there was not a urine test, blood test, or brain X-ray that determined their diagnoses. After explaining that most diagnoses are based primarily on symptoms reported to the therapists, I emphasize that if the behavioral symptoms diminish or disappear, the diagnosis may no longer be valid. For many clients, this information helps provide them with hope that a better life is possible.

With a reality therapy perspective, diagnoses are viewed as a symptom of a much larger problem: an inability to form healthy, need-satisfying relationships. Therefore, a choice theory/reality therapy perspective fosters a more "people first" approach in relating to clients. The diagnoses are viewed more as symptoms of the problem rather than causes. Unfortunately, those with a more limited understanding of choice theory/reality therapy sometimes have the misconception that this approach fosters victim-blaming. In actuality, the reality therapist helps empower the client. The reality therapist views clients as doing the best they can with the information that they currently possess. The therapist acts as a new source of information, which helps empower clients to have a more satisfying life.

Although mental illness diagnoses provide the benefit of a brief description of client behavioral symptoms, at times they seem to have questionable value in treatment planning. Yet, the use of diagnosis in treatment planning appears to be unlikely to change. This fact does not mean that choice theory/reality therapy treatment planning cannot be integrated into the *Diagnostic and Statistical Manual* treatment planning model. A reality therapist can view the DSM diagnoses of clients as the most recognizable parts of their total behavior. Next, the reality therapist can help find quality world pictures and basic needs related to the total behaviors. Frequently, team members are at odds about a client diagnosis yet are more often in agreement about the client's unmet needs, unsatisfied quality world pictures, and out-of-balance scales. In my opinion, this is true, because I believe quality world pictures and basic needs are more definable than mental illness diagnoses.

Another advantage is that choice theory language is more conducive to developing strength-based treatment goals and objectives. Thus, it makes sense, from a choice theory perspective, to use quality world pictures and basic needs as the diagnostic schema.

One of the main problems with today's treatment planning is that many of the stated goals and objectives in the treatment plans are not based on any real conceptualization of the client from a theoretical perspective. Because the treatment planning is not theory-driven, neither is the therapy. According to Jacobs (1994), counseling is most effective when it is theory-driven.

Reality therapy has a solid theory to justify the counseling process. In order to practice reality therapy most effectively, a clinician needs to have a good understanding of the theory behind the process. Choice theory is the basis of reality therapy. Choice theory is the brainchild of Dr. William Glasser. Glasser and G. L. Harrington developed the method of helping people known as reality therapy. According to Dr. Glasser (1998), human beings are motivated to follow "genetic instructions," which lead to fulfillment of the basic needs of survival, love/belonging, power, freedom, and fun. In addition to having healthy relationships with the important people in one's life, having some relative balance in these need areas leads to good mental health. Although having some balance is essential for good mental health, Glasser theorizes that the intensity levels of each need vary from individual to individual.

Since adequate need-fulfillment is a key to mental health, this may be an appropriate starting point for developing treatment plans. In other words, instead of using the client diagnoses as the central guiding mechanism in treatment planning, the reality therapist uses the five basic needs (survival, love/belonging, power/achievement, freedom, and fun) as a diagnostic schema and a starting point in assessing client strengths, areas of improvement, abilities, and preferences. With gathering this information, the reality therapist can more easily produce a treatment plan that is more individualized and practical.

One of our major dilemmas as human beings is that we cannot fulfill our needs directly. However, there is a more specific motivator of human behavior called our "wants" or "quality world pictures." Quality world pictures include desires and images that reflect how we want the external world to be. These pictures are the pathways through which we satisfy our internal basic needs. We have quality world pictures of important people like family and friends. A job/career might represent a pathway to a sense of power. We may have certain hobbies that give us a sense of fun or enjoyment. A favorite vacation spot may give us a sense of freedom (Glasser 1998; Glasser 2011).

The reality therapist accesses the client's world to gather the client's input for the treatment plan. Therefore, the reality therapist avoids "the expert" role of "telling the client like it is" or sending an "I know what is best for you" message. Instead, the reality therapist sees the client as "the expert" of his/her own quality world.

As human beings, we view the world through our perceptions. The information acquired through our five senses enters our total knowledge filter and then is assigned a label of positive, negative, or neutral when it enters the valuing filter (Glasser 1998).

Labeling is one of the negative side effects inherent in diagnosing. Unfortunately, labels, such as "bipolar" and "ADHD" and "psychotic" become part of the client's self-concept. Frequently, children and their families will define themselves by such labels. Thus, if a person sees himself as "bipolar," he is likely to generate behaviors congruent with that particular diagnosis. The reality therapist does not emphasize the diagnosis in his/her description of the client. Rather than saying, "He is an ADHD child," the reality therapist recognizes the client as primarily a human being by saying, "He is a child with a diagnosis of ADHD," or "He is a child exhibiting ADHD behaviors." This people-first perception increases the likelihood of the therapist treating the client with respect, because human beings tend to look for information to support current perceptions.

When we perceive that we are getting what we desire from the outside world, this consistency between our quality world and our perceived world gives us a sense of need-fulfillment. However, when we detect inconsistency between our quality world pictures and the perceived world, our behavioral system produces a frustration signal, which causes us to generate total behavior (Glasser 1998; 2011).

According to Glasser (1998; 2011), the behavior that we generate is total. Total behavior is comprised of: acting, thinking, feeling, and physiology. Using a car analogy, Glasser describes acting and thinking as the front wheels while feeling and physiology are the back wheels. Since we have more control over the acting and thinking wheels, this is the most logical place to begin when helping people make changes in their lives. These four components are inseparable; so if one changes a thought or action, the other components will also change with it. In essence: acting + thinking = feeling and physiology. Although the impact of the change in the acting and thinking wheels may not be immediately recognizable in the feeling and physiology wheels, they will eventually come along with it (Glasser 1998; Glasser 2011).

The behavioral system generates two types of behaviors: organized and reorganized. Organized behaviors are behaviors that have been used in the past for producing need-fulfillment. However, once these behaviors are no longer effective, new behaviors are created, which is called reorganizing. The reality therapist looks to build on strengths, so identifying effective, organized behaviors is crucial in treatment planning. If there are no effective organized behaviors present, the reality therapist will help the client reorganize or find new, more effective behaviors (Glasser 1998; Glasser 2011).

The concepts of organizing and reorganizing are very important in terms of the practice of RT. People do not change their behavior until they recognize the ineffectiveness of the choices they are making.

Consequently, people will continue less effective behaviors expecting a more positive result. This is why the procedure of self-evaluation is such an important part of RT. Once people have made the value judgment that their choices are not as effective as they would like, the process of reorganizing can begin. At this time, people will entertain the idea of new ways of thinking and acting (Glasser 1998, Glasser 2011).

The total behavior that originates inside of us has a purpose. The purpose is to impact the world around us so that we get the perception that there is consistency between our perceived world and our quality world (Glasser 2011). Dr. Robert E. Wubbolding (2011) adds another purpose of total behavior: "to send a message to the rest of the world." When a person enters counseling, usually one component of the total behavior is more recognizable than others. The more recognizable total behaviors will likely influence the diagnosis given to the client. Listed below are some examples:

Acting: Disruptive behavior disorders (ADHD and ODD) and substance abuse disorders

Thinking: Psychotic, cognitive, and impulse control disorders

Feeling: Affective disorders (bipolar and mood disorders) and anxiety disorders

Physiology: Somatoform disorders

In today's managed health care system, the clinician needs to ensure that treatment goals and objectives are related to the DSM diagnoses, which describe the client's total behaviors. Although reality therapists do not tend to emphasize diagnosing when working with the client, the diagnosis can be useful in summarizing many of the client's total behaviors.

In summary, human beings operate similarly to a negative feedback control system loop. For a more detailed description of choice theory, please refer to Dr. Glasser's book, *Choice Theory: A New Psychology of Personal Freedom.*

Chapter 2: Putting Choice Theory to Practice with Reality Therapy Treatment Planning

2. Putting Choice Theory to Practice with Reality Therapy Treatment Planning

A.   Emphasizing Relationships

Relationships are of primary importance in the practice of reality therapy. One of the best ways to describe the choice theory/reality therapy treatment planning perspective is client-focused. As stated previously, the reality therapist does not rely on the DSM diagnosis as the central guiding mechanism of treatment direction. Instead, the reality therapist relies on client input, especially input related to the client's quality world pictures. Reality therapists clarify and negotiate their role in helping by exploring client expectations as well as sharing their own. Reality therapists may ask, "Tell me what you would like to get from therapy. How will you know when you no longer need therapy? What would you like to see included as part of your treatment plan? How do you see me helping you?"

Glasser (1994) identifies six things other people must know about us before we can help them:

1. Who I am?
2. What I stand for?
3. What you can expect from me?
4. What to not expect from me?
5. What I will expect from you?
6. What I will not expect from you?

I have found these six questions to be very helpful in establishing and maintaining boundaries with clients as well as negotiating a defining role in helping. Glasser (1994) describes four relationships: friend to friend; manager to employee; counselor to client; and teacher to student. Although a therapist primarily functions in the counselor-to-client mode, the three other roles are important in order for the therapist to effectively help the client. These six questions are especially helpful when the therapist is in the managing role. In the appendix (pages 67-68), you will see an example of how these questions can be used to clarify roles and expectations in the therapy relationship.

With reality therapy, the counselor-client relationship is viewed as one of collaboration in which both parties are viewed as equals. Modeling what Dr. Glasser calls the "Seven Caring Habits" (supporting, accepting, trusting, listening, encouraging, respecting, and negotiating) is essential for the reality therapist to establish therapeutic conditions in order for the process to be effective (Glasser and Glasser, 2000).

The reality therapist listens for perceptual differences between what the clients want and have, which can be defined as the presenting issues bringing clients into treatment. Once the presenting problems are defined, the reality therapist may take a first step in treatment planning by reframing the presenting problems into potential solutions based on uncovering the quality world pictures tied to the presenting issues. For example, the client may state, "I cannot tolerate being disrespected by my peers." The reality therapist may paraphrase by saying, "It is important for you to be respected by your peers." The client acknowledges that the reality therapist's paraphrase was correct and knows that the therapist is in tune with the client's quality world. Furthermore, there is a subtle shift in the session from a problem-focused perspective to more of a solution-focused perspective, which helps create a more positive atmosphere in the therapy session.

B.   Focusing on Current Behavior

The reality therapist focuses on current behavior by exploring clients' actions, thoughts, feelings, and even their physiological symptoms. These components of total behavior are not dealt with in isolation from one another. Emphasis is placed on the acting and thinking components, because these two dimensions are more controllable. Reality therapists help clients in recognizing the inseparable relationship among the four components of total behavior by connecting what clients are doing and thinking with what they are feeling and their physiological symptoms. As a result, clients gain more awareness and control over their total behaviors.

Just like reality therapy, treatment planning emphasizes actions. This is mainly because actions are the easiest component of total behavior to measure. Examples of ways in which a reality therapist may explore total behavior include saying or asking: "Give me some examples of how you have tried to resolve your issue." Or, "How do you know when you are unhappy?" "When you are feeling happy, what are you doing?"

C.   Self-Evaluation in Treatment Planning

Robert E. Wubbolding describes self-evaluation as "the keystone in the arch" (2011) of the practice of reality therapy. In reality therapy, clients are continually encouraged to evaluate their progress toward treatment goals and objectives. They are also asked to evaluate and reevaluate their treatment plans. Some examples of self-evaluation questions and statements include: "Share your perception of what goals and objectives you have achieved and which ones you have not." "Are your current treatment goals and objectives realistic?" "Is your current treatment plan working for you?" "How committed are you to your treatment plan?"

In the appendix (page 71), you will see a diagram of the sandwich analogy used to illustrate the practice of reality therapy. Notice that the procedure of self-evaluation and the emphasis on relationships are the "buns" of the sandwich, which help to hold everything together. The emphasis on self-evaluation and relationships is what seems to separate reality therapy from other forms of cognitive-behavioral therapy. For more information on the procedure of self-evaluation, I recommend Dr. Robert E. Wubbolding's book, *Reality Therapy for the 21st Century,* in which he writes extensively about the different types of self-evaluation questions that can be used in therapy sessions with clients.

Action planning is less likely to be effective if the therapist skips the evaluation procedure of reality therapy. As previously stated, most people do not make changes until they have made the self-assessment that what they are doing is not working as effectively as they would like.

D.   Action Planning

Action planning is a central part of reality therapy. Wubbolding (2011) uses the acronym SAMIC to describe some of the major elements of an effective plan:

S = Simple
A = Attainable
M = Measurable
I = Immediate
C = Controlled by the planner

The aforementioned characteristics of an effective plan are very similar to the characteristics that most managed care organizations (MCOs) are requiring for treatment goals and objectives in order to authorize treatment services. Many MCOs use the SMART acronym to describe the characteristics of effective treatment goals and objectives. The SMART acronym stands for the following characteristics:

S = Specific
M = Measurable
A = Achievable
R = Results-Oriented
T = Time-Limited

Specific

Treatment outcome measures need to be specific in that they describe when, where, what, and how the progress with be measured. The more precise the outcome measure, the easier it will be to evaluate progress. Vague treatment outcomes, such as, "Client will improve self-esteem" are difficult to evaluate, because progress will be based on the subjective perceptions of treatment team members. Treatment team members are likely to disagree about whether the treatment outcomes have been achieved, which makes determining the end of service much more challenging. Debate among treatment team members about whether outcome measures have been achieved is often a sign that more specific treatment outcome measures are required. For clinicians who do not take treatment planning as seriously, treatment plans become useless documents that are, at best, remotely related to the therapy occurring in treatment sessions. With these clinicians, treatment outcomes are just something to look good on paper and are there primarily just to get services authorized. The treatment plan should be a clear road map for guiding the treatment team. Specific, individualized treatment plans demonstrate good outcome measures and client care.

Measurable

Logic tells us that runners are more likely to finish the race if they know where to find the finish line. Likewise, clients are more likely to achieve their treatment goals if they can easily measure their progress toward achieving them. Sometimes treatment outcomes are not written in a way that is easily measured. For example, consider the two following treatment outcome measures:

- Client will consume fruit eight out of ten times.
- Client will consume a serving of fruit at least two times per day for a period of one week.

Which is easier to measure? Obviously, the second outcome measure is much more specific and easier to track progress.

Clearly defining progress or a lack of progress will help validate the diligent work of clients and what they are doing to meet their goals. When progress is clearly defined, the treatment team can course correct, and there is opportunity to determine if the client is in the right level of care for treatment needs. Finally, measurable plans allow everyone the opportunity to celebrate steps to success regardless of how large or small they may be.

Achievable

To write an outcome measure like, "Client will lose forty pounds in one week" is not achievable unless the client is planning to have surgery.

Remember to assist clients in self-evaluating the achievability of their treatment goals and objectives. Unrealistic treatment outcomes can help set clients up for failure. Breaking tasks down into smaller, workable units is a way to make overwhelming obstacles more obtainable. By defining our success as taking one small step beyond where we are now, we are more likely to feel successful and less likely to feel discouraged. Please help clients develop achievable outcome measures that have a high probability of success.

Another example of treatment outcome measures that may not be measurable are those that focus totally on problem solving. Most people coming to therapy already know the solutions to their problems. What is the solution to drinking or eating too much? Stop drinking and eating too much. What is the solution to not having any friends? Be friendlier. What is the solution to loneliness? Go out and meet people. It is more likely that people coming to therapy may be in need of thinking and acting skills to solve their problems.

The ultimate goal of the reality therapist is to help clients develop skills to solve their own problems. Initially, this may puzzle some clients who expect to be told what to do and may ask how a skill-building treatment is going to solve the problem. My response to them has always been, "Do you want a solution to your problem, or do you want skills to solve your own problems?" Reality therapists are information providers and/or teachers of skills. They do not put Band-Aids on gushing wounds. So my suggestion is to develop skill-building treatment plans rather than problem solving treatment plans. Problems are not always solvable, but as clients develop skills they may be able to diminish the size of their problems. As therapists, we may not always be able to help our clients solve their problems, but we can almost always help them develop a skill or improve a relationship that may help diminish their problems.

Results-Oriented

Research indicates that when we tell someone not to do something, we may actually help increase the probability that the person will choose to do the forbidden action. Choice theory helps explain this phenomenon. Since all behavior is purposeful, when we focus on stopping a behavior, frustration is produced, because we are taking away a behavior that has been tied to our quality world. This lack of need-fulfillment produces a frustration signal, which causes us to search for replacement behaviors designed to satisfy the pictures in our quality world. Unless a replacement behavior can be found, we will likely resort back to the less effective behaviors we are trying to stop. Therefore, stopping without starting something new is unlikely to succeed. Instead of outcome measures like "Client will stop drinking," consider "Client will start going to AA."

In my opinion, positively stated goals increase the likelihood of success. When writing treatment plans and documenting progress, emphasize abilities rather than limitations, focusing on a person's achievements, creative talent, or skills. As reality therapists, we have to train ourselves to accomplish this task, because as choice theory explains, human beings are more aware of when their needs are not being met as opposed to when they are being met. The human body produces frustration signals when our behavioral system scales are out of balance.

Here are some examples of negatively stated outcome measures:

- Client will reduce punching holes in walls from five times weekly to two times weekly.
- Client will reduce suicide attempts from six times annually to two times annually.
- Client will not relapse for six months.
- Client will reduce aggressive outbursts from eight out of ten times to six out of ten times.

An example of a more positively stated outcome measure would be, "Client will maintain sobriety for at least a six-month duration." This example of an outcome measure is more positively stated, because it focuses on what to do rather than what not to do. Positively stated goals are very much in line with Dr. William Glasser's ideas of building on strengths rather than deficits.

In 1993, the Phoenix Suns possessed the best win/loss record in the National Basketball Association (NBA). On their way to the NBA finals that season, they faced the Los Angeles Lakers in the first round of a best of five series. During the first game of the series, the Suns played one of their most erratic games of the season, which resulted in a surprise defeat for the heavily favored Phoenix team. In preparation for game two, Phoenix coach Paul Westphal decided to have his team view the game film from game one with the hope that studying the film would help his players to correct their mistakes. However, the result was that the Suns played another erratic game, which resulted in back-to-back losses. Facing elimination from the NBA playoffs, coach Westphal decided to have his team study a film from one of their best performances of the season against the Los Angeles Lakers. His goal was to improve team performance by focusing on their successes rather than their failures. As a result, the Phoenix Suns won the next three games. They won the series and advanced to the next round of the NBA playoffs. This story illustrates how much more effective it can be to build on strengths rather than focusing on deficits.

Time-Limited

Just imagine how much less productive the human race would be if we were immortal. Deadlines and expiration dates are essential to keeping us focused and productive. Time-limited treatment outcome measures can help our clients and treatment team members be accountable when progress is not being made. One of the reasons that managed care organizations exist has been because some behavioral health clinicians have been negligent in establishing time-limited treatment outcome measures. Some of these clinicians have continued to seek the authorization of services by repeatedly submitting treatment requests until the funding sources eventually denied authorization. If these clinicians can be more proactive in setting time-limited treatment outcomes, it will be easier to get authorization of treatment for those who need it the most.

Failure to establish time-limited treatment outcomes often leads to fostering dependency relationships between clients and their service team members without observable progress. After twelve months of treatment with the same therapist, if the client needs the therapist as much or more than when services started, there may be an issue with the treatment plan.

Semantics have been one of the most confusing aspects in treatment planning. Many people use the terms "goals" and "objectives" interchangeably. In fact, various MCOs and reviewers may have different definitions for goals and objectives, so it is usually necessary to learn the definitions of various outcome measures from each specific funding source. What the MCO is calling a "goal" may be what you would refer to as an "objective." However, to bring more clarity and reduce confusion, I prefer to view goals as the outcome and the objectives as the steps in the goal-attainment process. I see action plans as a way to make progress toward the objectives. In summary, we make plans to achieve objectives. When we reach an objective, we are one step closer to goal attainment. My personal definition of a treatment goal is what progress the client will have achieved by the time services are ready to end. To assist clients in making plans, the reality therapist may ask:

- What will you do today to take a small step toward obtaining a treatment objective?
- How can you be more satisfied in reaching the goals and objectives in your treatment plan?

In the practice of reality therapy, the reality therapist will encourage self-initiated plans by the client. However, frequently clients may not have the information or the skills necessary to develop self-initiated plans, so the reality therapist can then help them search for organized behaviors that have been successful in the past. Some examples may be asking the client:

- Tell me about a time when you were successful in a similar situation.
- Who is someone you know that has been successful in a similar circumstance?

Occasionally, clients may not have any effective organized behaviors available to them. In these cases, the reality therapist may supply information. However, the reality therapist will ask the client's permission before supplying this information. This is one example of how information-giving differs from advice-giving.

Plan Sheet

Name _____ Counselor_____Date_____

Six Steps to Making a Good Plan

1. Simple: Not complicated, a small plan, not self-defeating.
2. Specific: As to what, when, where, how, etc.
3. A Do Plan: A "do something plan" as opposed to a "stop doing something plan"
4. Repetitive: Something you can do each day or repeat often.
5. Independent: A plan that is contingent or dependent only upon you and not upon others.
6. Immediate: A plan that can be started right away or real soon, a "now plan"

If you want to do better and feel better, start building some psychological strengths into your life. *Make a plan. Make a commitment, and put it into action now!*

The Five Basic Needs

1. Survival: Choose to practice good health.
2. Love/belonging: Choose to approach others first.
3. Power: Choose to achieve something each day.
4. Freedom: Choose to be responsible and see choices.
5. Fun: Choose to promote fun each day.

My plan is:

_____

_____

_____

_____

_____

When the plan is completed, circle "yes" or "no" beside each day of the week, and comment on how you feel.

Day Completed? Comments/Feelings

Sunday YES NO _____

Monday YES NO _____

Tuesday YES NO _____

Wednesday YES NO _____

Thursday YES NO _____

Friday YES NO _____

Saturday YES NO _____

I choose to be responsible and commit to the plan.

Client's signature _____

Chapter 3: Writing Treatment Goals and Objectives

3. Writing Treatment Goals and Objectives

When it comes to looking at most behaviorally based treatment planning, the identified problems are clearly stated, and the objectives are measurable. However, quite frequently this type of treatment planning is symptom-focused and does not address the underlying treatment issues. For example, a behavioral treatment plan may address the acting component of a client's total behavior but may not address the quality world pictures, perceptions, and unmet needs that are tied to the total behavior. The reality therapy treatment planning perspective provides a more holistic approach that goes beyond addressing the symptoms of problems. As Dr. William Glasser (1998) has stated, "Relationships are the root of most long-term psychological problems." From a reality therapy perspective, treatment goals and objectives focus on how people can improve their relationships with others as well as themselves and to more effectively meet their needs.

Before developing treatment goals and objectives, it is important to review some of the essential components of the treatment plan. Those components include symptoms/behaviors to be addressed, baseline measures, and strengths/natural supports.

The symptoms/behaviors to be addressed will include the total behaviors (acting, thinking, feeling, and physiology) related to the diagnosis, which will be targeted. Usually, the total behaviors that are most recognizable will be identified as the targeted symptoms. Clients with a diagnosis of oppositional defiant disorder (ODD) are more likely to have recognizable symptoms in the action component, such as fighting or truancy. On the other hand, clients with a diagnosis of mood disorder will have more noticeable symptoms in the feeling component, such as feelings of apathy or indifference. A client with a thought disorder may present less effective self-talk as a primary symptom. Finally, some clients may come to therapy via a physician referral because of some physical complaint that has no organic basis.

Baseline measures are important for establishing where the client is at the beginning of treatment in relation to the desired outcome. It is impossible to document progress accurately without some sort of starting point. For example, knowing that a client has a baseline of four hospitalizations within the past year due to suicidal behavior will provide much more meaning to a goal of a client having a period of six months without requiring hospitalization.

Since the early days of reality therapy, Dr. William Glasser has emphasized the importance of building on client strengths. Building on client strengths is a foundation of an effective treatment plan. In fact, many of the accrediting bodies of mental health agencies encourage that these be listed on the treatment plan. SNAP is an acronym for strengths, needs, abilities, and preferences, information that could be considered in the development of a treatment plan. Listed below is an example:

Strengths: Intelligent, articulate, and cooperative
Needs: Confidence and more social interaction
Abilities: Artistic and musical
Preferences: One-on-one interaction and reading

In summary, the targeted behaviors are identified, baseline measures recorded, and the strengths/needs/abilities/preferences are reviewed. Next, treatment goals and objectives are ready to be formulated. With mental health practitioners viewing their clients through a choice theory lens, treatment goals are related to the elements of choice theory/reality therapy. Generally, the objectives are related to quality world pictures, while the needs are more related to the goals. This makes sense, because it is through our quality world pictures that we satisfy our basic needs. It is through treatment objectives that we achieve our treatment goals. Goals and need-fulfillment are the outcomes while wants and objectives are the process.

Self-Preservation/Survival/Security/Health: The need for air, water, food, shelter, etc. It also refers to being mentally and physically in balance.

Examples of treatment goals related to Self-Preservation/Survival/Security/Health:

Goals:

1. Client will report a 10 to 15 percent improvement in overall health.
2. Client will reduce LDL level by 25 percent.
3. Client will increase HDL level 10 to 15 percent.
4. Client will lose ten pounds.
5. Client will document a 25 percent increase in activity level and maintain it for ninety consecutive days.
6. Client's lab report will show a 20 percent decrease in sodium.
7. Client's lab report will show a 25 percent increase in potassium.
8. Client will improve his/her overall score on wellness assessment by 10 to 15 percent.
9. Client will maintain current weight for at least ninety days.
10. Client will have a period of six months without an acid reflux attack.
11. Client will have at least seven bowel movements within one week.
12. Client will average logging at least seven hours of sleep for twenty-one consecutive days.
13. Client will express a desire to live by reporting a level of suicidal ideation that has dropped to zero.
14. Client will express hope for the future and verbalize a desire to live.
15. Client will be free of thoughts and feelings to inflict self-injury for at least seventy-two consecutive hours.
16. Client will develop a written safety plan.
17. Patient will be injury-free during hospitalization for three consecutive days.
18. Client will be free of manic symptoms for two consecutive months.
19. Client will show improved mental health as evidenced by a period of six months without requiring a hospital assessment.

Examples of treatment objectives related to Self-Preservation/ Survival/Security/Health:

Objectives:

1. Client will exercise for at least thirty minutes per day for one month.
2. Client will substitute water in place of soda for each meal for one week.
3. Client will evaluate problem areas in his/her life and list items over which he/she has control, influence, or no control.
4. Client will consume no more than 1200 calories per day for three consecutive months.
5. Client will make a list of a least five things she/he can do to improve her/his health.
6. Client will substitute fruit and vegetable snacks in place of sweets for one week.
7. Client will take a fifteen-minute walk either outside or in a public building each day for one month.
8. Client will explore four thoughts and feelings that lead to feeling out of control.
9. Client will complete a smoking cessation program.
10. Client will put his/her fork down on the table in between each bite of food.
11. Client will chew his/her food ten times before swallowing.
12. Client will sign and honor a contract to keep herself/himself safe for at least twenty-four hours.
13. Within the first three counseling sessions, client will explore the precipitants of self-injurious behavior.
14. Client will make a weekly action plan to improve his/her health for a period of one month.
15. Client will average eight hours of sleep for at least one week.
16. Client will achieve an HDL of at least forty.
17. Client will check his/her blood pressure two times per day for one month.
18. Client will weigh himself/herself each day for one month.
19. Client will have three servings of fruit or vegetables each day for thirty consecutive days.

20. Client will take ten thousand steps per day as measured by a pedometer for twenty-one consecutive days.
21. Client will practice relaxation techniques for thirty minutes each day.
22. Client will explore total behaviors (actions, thoughts, feelings, and physiological symptoms) related to suicidal ideation within two weeks.
23. Client will be able to identify at least three reasons to continue living.
24. Client will be able to externalize anger and direct it at appropriate objects within five weeks.
25. Client will plan three activities around positive life alternatives.
26. Client will discuss his/her desire to stop taking his/her medication with his physician.
27. Client will report any thoughts of self-harm to her/his clinician and identify two alternative ways of coping with such thoughts.
28. Patient will keep daily behavioral records of the frequency of self-destructive behavior for two consecutive weeks.
29. Client will identify and practice at least three new alternatives for dealing with self-aggressive impulses.
30. Client will maintain a weight of at least one hundred pounds.
31. Client will identify at least two quality world pictures and unmet needs associated with anorexic behaviors.
32. Client will identify at least one staff member whom he/she feels can be trusted.
33. Client will eat three meals a day for one week.
34. Client will identify at least three cognitive distortions related to acts of self-harm.
35. Client will describe at least two bodily sensations he/she observes when he/she is not angry as well as at least two bodily sensations he/she observes during an angry outburst.
36. Client will list at least three contacts in safety plan in case of suicidal thoughts/feelings.

Love/Belonging; The ability to connect with others, establish intimacy, or a sense of closeness with others.

Examples of treatment goals related to Love/Belonging:

Goal:

1. Client will report an improved relationship with at least three important people in his/her life.
2. Using Pete's Pathogram, client will report a 25 percent increase in her/his ability to satisfy her/his love/belonging needs.
3. Client will identify a meaning/purpose she/he has discovered during her/his grieving process.
4. Client will report improved relationships with her/his teachers.
5. Client will demonstrate the ability to control impulsive behavior as evidenced by zero reports of receiving in-house suspension at school.
6. Client will report better relationships with peers at school.
7. Client will memorize the "Seven Disconnecting Habits" and the "Seven Connecting Habits of Relationships."
8. Client will demonstrate replacing criticizing with supporting others in relationships while in the presence of staff in at least three different program areas.
9. Client will describe how he/she may substitute blaming with accepting others in relationships by listing five things he/she can do to show more acceptance of others.
10. Client will reduce complaining and increase ability to trust others. She/he will give three examples of ways she/he is conveying trust in others.
11. Client will be able to explain the difference between nagging and encouraging to at least two different service team members.
12. Client will show how to replace three threatening behaviors with three respecting behaviors in relating with others during family sessions.

13. Client will avoid punishing by demonstrating use of five different negotiation skills during in-home family therapy sessions.
14. Client will demonstrate how he/she can replace bribing with three newly acquired supportive behaviors during family therapy sessions.
15. Family will utilize the solving circle to resolve three family conflicts.
16. Client will report a 30 percent increase in confidence in relating to the opposite sex.
17. Client will identify a newly formed intimate relationship.
18. Client will describe three to five times in which he/she demonstrated an ability to express affection effectively.
19. Client will complete a weekly journal for three months on his/her perception of his/her interactions with other people.

Objectives:

1. Client will explore the unmet needs in each of the important relationships in his/her life.
2. Client will discuss the satisfied and unsatisfied pictures of his/her relationships with the important people in his/her life.
3. Client will explore his/her perception of his relationship with each of the important people in his/her life.
4. Client will spend at least thirty minutes in a public setting one time each week for one month.
5. Client will engage in people-watching for at least fifteen minutes each week for one month.
6. Client will identify the eye color of at least three different people.
7. Client will say hello first to at least one person each day for one week.
8. Client will smile and say hello first to at least three different people.
9. Client will smile, say hello first, and include the person's name in the greeting.
10. Client will develop at least three opening statements/questions to start conversations with others.

11. Client will share at least one interesting fact about herself/himself to each new person she/he meets within the next thirty days.
12. Client will identify at least three ways to say "I love you" without words.
13. Client will practice giving specific compliments during role-plays with therapist each session.
14. Client will give three specific compliments to other people within one week.
15. Client will contact a friend with whom she/he has lost contact.
16. Client will memorize the "Seven Deadly Relationship Habits" and the "Seven Caring Relationship Habits."
17. Client will identify her/his most frequently used deadly habits and make a plan to replace them with at least one of the caring habits.
18. Client will discuss at least one thing she/he can do to move closer to each of the important people in her/his life.
19. Client will memorize the characteristics of quality time.
20. Client will practice at least twenty minutes of quality time with at least one immediate family member each week.
21. Client will use an encouraging phrase with at least one person each day for one week.
22. Client will describe a time in her/his life when she/he had a strong sense of love/belonging in her/his life.
23. Client will list five ways he/she is currently demonstrating caring to others.
24. Client will discuss at least three ways she/he can be a positive role model to other women.
25. Client will discuss how she/he would like other people to see her/his and compare this perception to how she/he thinks they see her/his.
26. Client will develop a list of people to contact when she/he is experiencing unwanted feelings.
27. During three different sessions, client will discuss her/his progress with substituting the seven disconnecting habits with the seven connecting habits in her/his important relationships.

28. Client will describe three occasions in which she/he said "I love you" without words.
29. Client will list five to ten newly acquired social skills and demonstrate them at the next service team meeting.
30. Client will report at least a 5 to 10 percent improvement in a relationship with a family member or friend.
31. Client will memorize the guidelines for entering the solving circle.
32. Client will describe at least three times that she/he successfully used the solving circle to resolve a conflict.
33. Each session, client will practice self-evaluating the impact his/her decisions have on his/her relationships with the important people in his/her life for a time period of one month.
34. Client will practice starting a conversation with others at least twice per day for one week.
35. Client will talk about her/his feelings of grief with (name of person) related to losing her/his husband.
36. Client will practice countering negative self-statements by completing a daily monitoring form for one month.
37. Client will be able to recognize and identify three to five conflict-resolution styles and discuss the benefits and costs of each.
38. Client will identify three qualities he/she would like in a friend.
39. Client will initiate at least one conversation each day for one week.
40. Client will identify three antecedents to disruptive behavior.
41. Each session client will practice summarizing every fifteen minutes.
42. Client will be able to verbalize at least two functions of his/her anger and how they impact the relationships with the important people in his/her life.
43. Client will read a book about choice theory and identify at least three things ideas he/she will use in order to strengthen a relationship.

Power/Achievement/Self-Worth/Inner Control: To be competent, self-actualized, to possess self-esteem, or to have recognition.

Examples of treatment goals related to Power/Achievement/Inner Control/Recognition:

Goals:

1. Client will have increase self-worth, self-control, and self-esteem as evidenced by increasing self-concept questionnaire survey score from twenty-four to at least sixty-one.
2. Patient will increase his/her participation in milieu activities as evidenced by completing all assigned duties.
3. Client will memorize four simple questions to ask himself/herself before engaging in impulsive behavior.
4. Client will improve task completions by finishing three achievement plans.
5. Client will obtain GED.
6. Client will maintain on-task behavior and will engage in thoughtful (versus impulsive) decision making as evidenced by using the WDEP (W = What do you **W**ant? What are you **D**oing? **E**valuate: Is it working? **P**lan: What can you do differently?) questioning process with at least three people on three different occasions.
7. Client will report having a relative perception of self and demonstrate behavior consistent with adequate self-esteem as well as exhibit less preoccupation with his own appearance.
8. Client will maintain passing grades in each of his/her courses for at least one semester.
9. Client will be able to identify his/her feelings of anger in at least three different program areas when prompted by staff.
10. Client will demonstrate by his/her actions that he/she is able to remain nonviolent when he/she feels anger.
11. Patient will achieve and maintain remission of hallucinations and delusions for a period of at least ninety consecutive days.
12. Client will eliminate physical aggression.

13. By using a subjective units of distress scale (SUDS), client will report a 50 percent improvement in his/her ability to manage anxiety.
14. Patient will be oriented to name, place, and time for at least three consecutive weekly sessions.
15. Client will eliminate constant depressive state for a period of at least thirty days.
16. Client will show improved anger management skills by replacing aggressive outbursts with nonaggressive conflict-resolution skills for a period of twenty-one consecutive days.
17. Using Pete's Pathogram, client will show a 15 percent improvement in his/her ability to satisfy his/her need for power/achievement/self-worth.
18. Client will show improvement with his/her ability maintain focus and manage his/her emotions as evidenced by at least one period of seventy-two hours without an episode of an angry outburst.

Objectives:

1. Client will memorize at least five elements of a good plan.
2. Client will commit to at least one action plan per week.
3. Each session client will identify two areas of achievement and one area to be improved.
4. Client will share her/his greatest achievements in her/his professional and personal life.
5. Client will identify at least three to five things he/she could do that would give him/her a sense of achievement.
6. Client will develop an action plan without the assistance of his/her therapist.
7. Client will follow through with three achievement plans within one week.
8. Client will completely revise and update his/her résumé.
9. Each week client will make at least three job contacts.
10. For a history class, client will read each textbook chapter three times.
11. For one week, client will remember to bring pencil and paper to each class.

12. Client will invite three people to join his/her weekly study group.
13. Client will prepare a practice test before each exam.
14. Client will complete a task that she/he has been putting off.
15. Client will stay on task for least fifteen minutes for three consecutive weekly play therapy sessions.
16. Client will list twenty-five of her/his positive attributes (five in each category: physical, emotional, behavioral, intellectual, and environmental).
17. Client will practice one technique that might improve her/his job skills for fifteen minutes each day for twelve out of fourteen days.
18. Client will identify three anger triggers.
19. Client will develop an action plan to cope with each anger trigger.
20. Client will practice at least one new relaxation technique during each session for six weeks.
21. Client will use behavioral rehearsal to practice assertion skills at least one time per session for six weeks.
22. Client will attend ninety AA meetings in ninety days.
23. Client will complete a twelve-week choice theory focus group.
24. Client will maintain sobriety for at least three consecutive months.
25. Client will describe his/her total behavior when recalling a time when he/she felt successful.
26. Client will describe his total behavior when he/she visualizes himself/herself as being successful.
27. Client and therapist will explore social/situational anger triggers. Client will identify/verbalize at least five anger triggers.
28. Client and therapist will discuss anger management techniques. He/she will acquire at least three to five new ways to effectively manage his/her anger. He/she will be able to verbalize and demonstrate at least three to five newly acquired skills to his/her therapist.
29. Client will memorize four simple questions to ask himself/herself to help him/her remember to use his/her coping skills.

30. Client will read a book about choice theory and describe three ways he/she can improve the quality of his/her life.

Freedom/Independence/Autonomy: The ability to move and choose or to stand on one's own feet.

Examples of treatment goals related to Freedom/Independence/ Autonomy:

Goals:

1. Client will increase her/his level autonomy, freedom, and independence by obtaining a driver's license.
2. Client will become more self-sufficient by holding a job for at least six months.
3. Client will demonstrate ten new coping skills to manage his/her emotions.
4. Client will report improving her/his self-talks.
5. Client will embrace fifteen minutes of solitude time each day for a period of thirteen weeks in order to improve her/his mental health.
6. Client will be able to develop his/her own achievement plans.
7. Client will be able to sleep in his/her own bed.
8. Client will draw three alternate strategies for managing her/his anxiety.
9. Client will develop sufficient computers skills to obtain employment.
10. Client will accept more responsibility for his/her actions by replacing his/her three favorite excuses with "I" statements.
11. Client will demonstrate the ability to rethink rather than react by teaching the questioning process of reality therapy to at least three different people.
12. Client will improve independent decision-making skills by reporting three difference occasions in which he/she resolved conflict without violence.
13. Client will be able to resist negative peer pressure for a period of three months as reported and documented by client and service team.

14. Client will learn to self-evaluate, self-monitor, and self-regulate his/her behavior by graduating an anger-management program.
15. Using Pete's Pathogram, client will report at least a 12 percent increase in her/his ability to fulfill her/his need for freedom/autonomy/independence.
16. Using a subjective units of distress (SUD) scale, client will report a 25 percent improvement in managing her/his level of anxiety.
17. Client will show improved mental health as evidenced by a child post-traumatic stress scale (CPSS) score no higher than fourteen.

Objectives:

1. Client will identify the rules she/he lives by.
2. Client will develop a list of rules and consequences to be followed at home.
3. Client will write a list of things he/she feels he/she has to do or should do and then write a new list replacing each "have to" and "should" with "choosing" or "I want.
4. Client will list things she/he does not have to do, nor want to do. She/he will then shed the list and make a commitment to focus on a new list comprised of the things she/he feels she/he has to do or wants to do.
5. Client will identify three characteristics he/she does not like about himself/herself and then name at least one positive about each thing.
6. Client will give himself/herself permission to feel unhappy for fifteen minutes each day and then will make an action plan to help himself/herself feel better.
7. Client will self-evaluate the positive choices she/he has made the previous week during each session for six consecutive weeks.
8. Client will be able to develop an action plan without the assistance of someone else.
9. Client will allow herself/himself thirty minutes of downtime each day.

10. Client will identify his/her top three excuses that prevent him/her from becoming more independent in decision-making.
11. Client will describe his total behavior regarding activities and places that give him/her an added sense of freedom and independence.
12. For a duration of three weeks, client will practice a new conflict-resolution skill (in role-plays with therapist) to give her/his new choices in handling disagreements with others.
13. Client will track his/her daily anger outbursts on a monthly calendar.
14. Client will describe how her/his medication impacts her/his actions, thoughts, feelings, and physiology.
15. Client will complete a trauma narrative regarding past abuse and identify three things she/he has learned from the experience that will benefit her/his in the present and future.

Fun/Enjoyment: To increase level of fun/enjoyment in ways that do not lead to getting in trouble. Learning something new can also be a part of this need.

Examples of treatment goals related to Fun/Enjoyment" and "Examples of treatment objectives related to Fun/Enjoyment:

Goals:

1. Client will report an increased level of enjoyment by taking a vacation.
2. Client will replace feelings of boredom with enjoyment for a period of two weeks by reporting three things he/she accomplished that brought him/her a sense of joy.
3. Client will be able to entertain self for thirty days without depending upon others.
4. Client will increase pathways for putting fun into his/her life by identifying three places to go for enjoyment that are legal and not harmful to him/her or the significant people in his/her life.
5. Client will increase ability to see humor by identifying three areas of his/her life that he/she is taking too seriously.

6. Client will identify a total of at least ten new ways of having fun at home, work, and in the community.
7. Client will demonstrate at least five new fun-making skills.
8. Client will practice five new ways of having fun that are legal.
9. Client will learn to gain a sense of enjoyment without the assistance of drugs as reported by client.
10. Client will memorize the characteristics of quality time.
11. Using Pete's Pathogram, client will show at least an 18 percent improvement in her/his ability to satisfy her/his need for fun/enjoyment.
12. Client will show at least a 5 percent decrease in depressive symptoms based on her/his Beck Depression Inventory (BDI) score.

Objectives:

1. Client will list and discuss ways she/he is currently meeting her/his need for fun.
2. Client will identify at least three things she/he used to do for fun that she/he wishes she/he was still doing.
3. Client will identify at least three new ways of putting fun into her/his life without getting in trouble.
4. Client will invite a friend to do something fun each week for thirty days.
5. Client will find at least one new hobby and give himself/herself thirty to sixty minutes each week to engage in the hobby for one month.
6. Client will discuss at least one way he/she has experienced fun by himself each week for thirty days.
7. Client will discuss at least one way he/she had fun with others each week.
8. Client will start a joke file and collect at least ten jokes.
9. Client will learn at least three to five magic tricks to show others.
10. Client will make a plan to do something fun in each of his/her environments (home, work, church, etc.)
11. Client will read the newspaper each day.
12. Client will complete an educational course of her/his choosing.

13. Client will attend weekly guitar lessons for thirteen weeks.
14. Client will read a self-help book and discuss three to five things that he/she learned or relearned.
15. Client will make a list of at least twenty things he/she can do for fun that are fun and do not lead to trouble.
16. Client will identify three less effective self-talk statements that prevent him/her from enjoying life more fully.
17. Client will replace less effective self-talk statements with at least three more effective self-talk statements.

In writing treatment goals/objectives related to the basic needs, please keep in mind that the basic needs overlap. Therefore, a single objective may be related to more than one quality world picture as well as more than one need. The only time we can separate the basic needs is when we teach them. Please remember to develop the treatment plans with the clients. It is essential to have the client present in order for the plans to be truly client-focused. What might be a goal for one client may be better written as an objective for another. Remember that the goals are the outcome of therapy while objectives are the process to achieving it.

Chapter 4: Writing Treatment Interventions

4. Writing Interventions Treatment Interventions

Treatment objectives are frequently confused with treatment interventions. While treatment goals and objectives describe what the client is going to do, interventions describe how the counselor/therapist will assist the client. Listed below and on the next page are some examples of interventions a therapist may use to assist a client.

Activity
1. Exploration of actions
2. Assessing level of commitment
3. Action planning
4. Assertion training
5. Conflict resolution
6. Systematic desensitization
7. Modeling
8. Behavioral rehearsal
9. Relaxation training
10. Allowing natural consequences
11. Imposing logical consequences
12. Envisioning
13. Invivo mastering
14. Safety planning
15. Successive approximations

Cognitive
1. Assessing locus of control
2. The mirror technique

3. Prioritizing goals
4. Reframing
5. Positioning
6. Restraining
7. Predicting relapse
8. Challenging less effective self-talk
9. Guided imagery
10. Cognitive processing and restructuring
11. Cost/benefit analysis
12. Coping cards
13. Psychoeducation

Affective
1. Reflection of feeling
2. Reflection of meaning
3. Empathic responses
4. Empty-chair technique
5. Dialogue of polarities
6. Affective modulation

Physiological
1. Biofeedback

Miscellaneous
1. Silence
2. Simple minimal verbal response
3. Accenting
4. Paraphrasing
5. Reflection
6. Summarization
7. Exploration
8. Questioning
9. Confronting
10. Educating
11. Immediacy
12. Use of humor
13. Storytelling
14. Play therapy

15. Role reversal
16. Contracting
17. Focusing
18. Funneling
19. Clarifying
20. Assigning homework
21. Bibliotherapy
22. Negotiating
23. Accepting
24. Active listening
25. Supporting
26. Trusting
27. Respecting
28. Journaling
29. Evoking
30. Affirming
31. Suggesting
32. Assessing
33. Limit-setting
34. Informing
35. Teaching
36. Instructing

Many mental health providers are required to write treatment interventions. Traditionally, interventions have been based on the carrot-and-stick external control philosophy of behavior modification in which it is believed that if one provides the proper stimulus, a person will elicit a desired response. Usually, these approaches utilize praise or rewards for "good" behavior and criticism or punishment for "bad" behavior.

Although these approaches can be quite effective for producing temporary compliance, they do little to promote cooperation and intrinsic motivation.

Before deciding on an intervention for a client, I think it is important to ask ourselves about our goals for this particular client. Are we looking for cooperation or temporary compliance? What message will we be encouraging or teaching with our interventions?

The problem with punishment/criticism is that it only teaches, "Don't misbehave because you might get in trouble." The client learns to be sorry for getting caught rather than learning about the impact his/her behavior has on others.

Rewards and praise seems to teach, "Do something positive, because other people will like you and may give you things." This frequently leads the client to develop conditions of worth and become overly dependent upon approval from others.

Perhaps there is another method to determine interventions that encourages cooperation and self-respect using less controlling and noncritical methods. This approach is based on Dr. William Glasser's choice theory. The choice theory approach to developing treatment interventions goes beyond focusing on antecedents, behavior, and consequences. I have formulated a description of how this approach could be implemented using the first seven letters of the alphabet.

Antecedents = What activating events led to the targeted total behaviors?
Behaviors = What components are most recognizable? What interventions have been used to manage the targeted total behaviors?
Consequences = What are the results of the targeted total behaviors?
Determine the goal of the targeted behavior = What quality world picture is tied to the targeted total behaviors?
Evaluation = What interventions have been effective or ineffective?
Find a more effective intervention = What interventions may work best?
Goal = Assist the client in setting a new treatment goal and objectives.

In the next two chapters the reader will have the opportunity to see how the choice theory/reality therapy treatment planning model can be applied to real-life cases. The chapters will illustrate the practical application of developing a treatment plan and the documentation of progress.

Chapter 5: Documentation of Progress Notes

5. Documentation of Progress Notes

Looking back at my graduate-level training in counseling and my supervision of students, I believe that training in treatment planning and documentation were underemphasized. Since much of the work of mental health professionals is behind closed doors, the only evidence of our work that others may see is our documentation. Poor documentation can often be a reason for mental health professionals to lose jobs or have their licenses suspended.

Documentation is also important for tracking progress toward treatment goals and objectives. Treatment plans should be reviewed each session. The progress note is a report on what progress has been made toward the treatment objectives and goals. I learned acronyms like SOAP (Subjective, Objective, Assessment, Plan) and DAP (Data, Assessment, Plan) in graduate school. Although these acronyms are helpful, I have put together my own acronym, because it helps to remember the importance of including documentation of the goals for the sessions as well as the interventions. Generally, mental health professionals do a pretty good job of documenting what their clients say and do. Where they are more likely to come up short is in documenting their interventions. It is just as important for clinicians to document how they helped clients as it is to document clients' observed symptoms. My own acronym is GDIP.

GDIP is a simple acronym used to remember the elements of effective documentation:

G = Goal: Identify the purpose of the session, including what the helper hoped to accomplish.

D = **D**ata: Describe the dimensions of the client's total behaviors that are most recognizable, including actions, cognitions, emotions, and physiological symptoms.

I = **I**nterventions: Document the actions the helper took to help the client.

P = **P**rogress: Note progress made toward treatment goals and objectives.

P = **P**lan: Write the plan for the next session.

Listed below are some examples.

Example #1

The goal of today's session was to explore and clarify the client's expectations of services. Client stated that he was referred for services due to experiencing severe depression and depression-related feelings like apathy and indifference. According to the client, his depression has had a negative impact on his relationships at home and at school. Counselor used open-ended questions to explore client's perception of the type of help he needs and to negotiate a role in helping the client. Client stated that he needs a coach to help him get back on the right track. He continued by saying he would like to understand what is causing his depression and how to effectively deal with it. Counselor assured client that he could be of assistance to him. Some progress noted regarding client being able to express his unmet needs more assertively. Next session will focus on helping client explore the connection between his thoughts/feelings and unmet needs.

Example #2

The goal of today's session was to teach client some new techniques for managing anxiety. At the beginning of the session, client rated her anxiety level as a 9 on a 0–10 scale, with 10 being the highest. According to the client, accompanying her feelings of anxiety were physiological symptoms (muscle tension and a mild headache) and thoughts of "wanting to avoid all the stress in her life." Therapist taught client the relaxation technique of stomach breathing (to replace chest breathing) and guided imagery to cope more productively with less effective self-talk. By the end of the session, client reported that her anxiety level had reduced to a 4 on the 0–10 scale. Some progress noted regarding client learning more effective coping skills. Next session therapist and client will address improving self-talk.

Example #3

Client began the session by reporting that he is feeling highly discouraged following his relapse after a three-month period of sobriety. According to the client, he believes his relapse was triggered following several job turn-downs. Client indicated that he feels like a "complete failure" for having relapsed following three months of sobriety. The goal of this session was to assist client in reframing failure as a potential stepping-stone to success. Therapist used reframing to help client recognize that three months of sobriety is at least a partial success and that occasional relapses can be an expected part of recovery. To cope with his perceived trigger for the relapse, therapist used reframing by helping the client see that with each turn-down, he is one step closer to finding the right job. By the end of the session, the client reported feeling somewhat encouraged. Next session therapist will provide client with information on how to use the elements of effective plan making in putting distance between relapses.

Hypothetical Example of a Crisis Intervention Note

Client: Jackson

The goal of this session was to assess the lethality of Jackson's suicidal ideation and his ability to cope with the recent loss of his spouse. Jackson reported feeling depressed, worthless, and lonely. Accompanying these feelings were thoughts of suicide and pessimism. Although he does not have a history of suicide attempts or a concrete plan, he reports feeling confident in his decision to take his own life.

Jackson's negative symptoms seem to be related to an unmet need for love/belonging, which has gone unmet since his wife passed away. He reports his wife as being his only connected relationship. Without a sense of belonging or a connection in his life, Jackson states that he sees life as meaningless.

To explore the purpose of Jackson's threat, therapist asked Jackson what he expected to happen when he told his therapist about making a decision to kill himself. Jackson acknowledged remembering the discussion from the initial session about the duty to warn and protect as well as the limitations of confidentiality. He also acknowledged that he suspected his therapist would be legally and ethically obligated to intervene. Following this gentle confrontation, Jackson agreed that he has some ambivalence about wanting to live or die. Therapist used self-evaluation questions to help Jackson examine the connection between his desires and behavior. Jackson made the self-assessment that it would be in his best interest to delay carrying out the decision to take his own life.

Jackson agreed to develop a safety plan. He also agreed to be admitted to a crisis stabilization unit. Therapist will contact the CSU therapist to arrange a transition planning conference next week.

Safety Planning

For many years, no-suicide contracts were a standard practice in handling suicidal threats and behaviors. In more recent times, there has been a shift from no-suicide contracts to safety planning. On the next page is an example of a safety plan that has many of the needed elements necessary to help ensure someone's safety, especially those behavioral health professionals working from a reality therapy perspective.

First, there is a section on the safety plan to identify warning signs by categorizing them into total behaviors. Occasionally, it may be helpful to remind clients that the acting warning signs are usually the signs of which they are least aware and may sometimes need help from others in recognizing and understanding. On the other hand, the warning signs categorized under feelings may sometimes be their best friends, because they are usually the first signs they notice when their scales are out of balance.

Second, the coping strategies section provides information to help determine some of the organized behaviors that have been effective for clients as well as some possible new strategies/behaviors that may help in the future. Having this information documented and visible to clients helps make the information easier for them to access in times of an impending crisis.

Third, the safety plan includes a place for ideas about how to create a safe environment. Any environmental change that can prevent access to a weapon, drugs, or other means reduces lethality.

Finally, I believe one of the most important sections of the safety plan is the "Things that are important to me" list, where clients list the things they feel are most important to them and worth living for in the future. Frequently, those who may be exhibiting suicidal behaviors are ambivalent about whether to continue living. As choice theory explains, human beings are more aware of when their quality world pictures are unsatisfied than when they are satisfied. Therefore, we can sometimes become so focused on negativity that we may forget about the blessings in our lives. The "Things that are important to me" list can help clinicians begin to access client quality world pictures, which helps get them in touch with the part of the client that still wants to live. Plus, the "Things that are important to me" list is a good assessment tool. If a client cannot come up with anything to put on this list, lethality greatly increases.

Safety Plan

Warning Signs
1. Acting:
2. Thinking:
3. Feeling:
4. Physiology:

Coping Strategies
1. Identify what has helped you in the past:
2. List some strategies you would be willing to do:
3. List some people and social settings that provide distraction:
4. People whom I can ask for help:
5. Professionals or agencies I can contact during a crisis:

Suicide prevention lifeline phone: 1-800-273-TALK (8255)
The Trevor Lifeline phone (gay or lesbian issues): 1-866-488-7386

Creating a Safe Environment
1. _____
2. _____

Things That Are Important to Me

List the things that are most important to me and worth living for:
1. _____
2. _____
3. _____

Chapter 6: Case Examples

6. Case Examples

Client #1: Walter

Walter is a seventeen-year-old male diagnosed with a social anxiety disorder. His parents have referred him for treatment due to his extreme shyness. He reports feeling very lonely and complains of not having any friends. His relationship with his parents appears to be pretty good. Walter seems to have a clear preference for introversion and admits that his mother or father usually act as his "spokesperson." Although Walter appreciates being the only child, he sometimes gets annoyed with his mother always "being in my business" and making decisions for him.

Treatment Plan

Name: Walter
Therapist: Mike Fulkerson, MAE, LPCC, CT/RTC
Strengths: Supportive family and desire to cooperate with others.
Needs: Social skills, confidence, and friends.
Abilities: Articulate, intelligent, and insightful.
Preferences: One-to-one interaction, writing, and reading.
Input from client: Walter states that he wants to overcome feelings of loneliness.

Problem #1:	Social anxiety disorder
Targeted behaviors:	An inability to establish and maintain friendships. Walter reports a high level of anxiety when around other people. He reports avoiding approaching other people first for fear of rejection and avoids making eye contact.

Baseline:	Walter reports having zero friends at school and at home.
Goal #1:	Walter will be able to identify the names of at least two people he considers to be a friend.
Objective #1:	Walter will spend at least thirty minutes in a public setting one time per week for at least two consecutive weeks.
Objective #2:	Walter will engage in people-watching for a minimum of fifteen minutes for at least two consecutive weeks.
Objective #3:	Walter will identify the eye color of at least three different people.
Objective #4:	Walter will say hi first to at least three different people without the expectation of his greeting being returned.
Objective #5:	Walter will develop at least four questions or statements with which to begin conversations.
Modalities:	Individual therapy one hour per week.
Interventions:	Relaxation techniques, assertion training, action planning, successive approximations, behavioral rehearsal, and cognitive processing.
Target date:	Nine months.

One of the important ideas to remember in treatment planning is to keep it as simple as possible. Also, it is important to remember to start where the client is and not where you are. If the therapist suggests to a very shy client like Walter that he just go out and meet people, this suggestion would be very foolish. Walter does not have the skills yet to be successful with this task. The therapist helps Walter take baby steps, which will be less likely to set Walter up for failure. Effective treatment planning provides clients with a high probability of success.

Client #2: Tonya

Tonya is a thirty-year-old female who has been diagnosed with bipolar disorder. Her mother has custody of Tonya's child due to Tonya's instability in relationships and with holding onto jobs. Tonya reports that she has noticed increased feelings of depression because she has not been able to find a job. She says that she feels very discouraged and is at a loss for what to do. Tonya has a history of having poor relationships with her work supervisors and has not been able to hold a job longer than three months. She blames having poor supervisors for her inability to keep jobs.

Treatment Plan

Name: Tonya
Therapist: Mike Fulkerson, MAE, LPCC, CT/RTC
Strengths: Extraverted, outspoken, demonstrative
Needs: Conflict-resolution skills and increased internal locus of control
Abilities: Creative and resilient
Preferences: Visual learner
Input from client: Tonya said she would like to maintain a job by learning how to deal with difficult people

Problem #1:	Bipolar disorder
Targeted behaviors:	Instability at work and in relationships.
Baseline:	Tonya has been unable to hold a job for longer than three months. She has made one job contact within the past month.
Goal #1:	Tonya will maintain a job for at least six months.
Objective #1:	Tonya will make at least three job contacts per week for a duration of least six weeks.
Objective #2:	Tonya will memorize four simple questions to ask herself to help her remember to use her coping skills.
Objective #3:	Tonya will be able to identify and demonstrate at least three new conflict-resolution skills in the presence of her therapist.
Modalities:	Individual therapy one hour per week.

Interventions:	Therapist will assist Tonya in learning to reframe her perceived failures as stepping-stones to success. Therapist will also teach Tonya how to use the questioning process of reality therapy as a self-help method. Role-plays will be used to teach conflict-resolutions skills.
Target date:	Six months.

Client #3: Juan

Juan is a seventeen-year-old male who was referred for treatment by his mother who reports that her son has been exhibiting fluctuations in his mood as well as verbal and physical aggression at home, school, and the community. Although Juan reports wanting to have a good relationship with his mother, he describes his interactions with her as stressful. Juan's father is not involved in his life. According to Juan's mother, Juan's father was physically abusive to both Juan and her. Juan's mother reports regretting that her son does not have a positive male role model in his life.

When asked for input regarding his treatment plan, Juan voices much frustration about his mother's tendency to be overly controlling. Juan reports wanting to obtain a driver's license but laments that his mother is "not letting me drive." During the first session, Juan and his mother agree to the following treatment plan.

Treatment Plan

Name: Juan
Therapist: Michael Fulkerson, MAE, LPCC, CT/RTC
Strengths: Outspoken, extraverted, kind, and generous
Needs: Increased self-control and decision-making skills
Abilities: Athletic skills and intelligence
Preferences: Sports, music, and art
Input from client: "I want help dealing with my anger."

Problem #1:	Disruptive mood dysregulation disorder (DMDD)

Targeted behaviors:	Inability to control emotions as evidenced by verbal and physical aggression at home, school, and the community.
Baseline:	Juan's lack of control and aggression has led to his mother's refusal to permit him to obtain his driver's license or permit.
Goal #1:	Juan will demonstrate increased control over his emotions by eliminating aggression and obtaining a driver's license.
Objective #1:	Juan will journal what he is doing, thinking, feeling, and describe his physiological symptoms in at least four consecutive therapy sessions.
Objective #2:	Juan will explain how his actions, thoughts, feelings, and physiology are similar to the functioning of a car.
Objective #3:	Juan will list at least three ways to manage his emotions more effectively.
Objective #4:	Juan will obtain his driver's permit.
Modalities:	Individual therapy for at least one hour per week.
Interventions:	Therapist will introduce client to the basic concepts of choice theory and assist client in using reality therapy as a self-help method.
Target date	Nine weeks.

Problem #2:	Anxiety disorder
Targeted behaviors:	Negative self-talk, giving up easily, and frequent pacing.
Baseline:	Juan scored 30 on the self-concept questionnaire. Scores below 60 are considered low.
Goal #1:	Juan will achieve a self-concept questionnaire score of at least 61.
Objective #1:	Juan will identify three new relaxation skills and demonstrate these in the presence of his therapist.
Objective #2:	Juan will be able to list at least fifteen of his positive attributes.
Objective #3:	Juan will identify at least five positive characteristics of the person he most admires.

Objective #4:	Juan will commit to at least three achievement plans to be more like the person he most admires.
Objective #5:	Juan will report achieving each of his three achievement plans to be more like the person he admires most.
Interventions:	Cognitive restructuring will be used to assist client in thinking differently about himself and his environment. Reframing will be used to assist in recognizing strengths, especially those that he perceives as weaknesses.
Modalities:	Individual therapy for one hour per week.
Target date:	Nine weeks.

Problem #3:	Parent-child relational problem
Targeted behaviors:	Juan and his mother report that their interactions usually involve arguing, blaming, and criticizing each other.
Baseline:	Both Juan and his mother report feeling dissatisfied with their relationship.
Goal #1:	Both Juan and his mother will report feeling satisfied with their relationship.
Objective #1:	Juan and his mother will come to an agreement regarding the rules and consequences to be followed at home.
Objective #2:	Both Juan and his mother will identify three positive results from replacing disconnecting relationship habits with connecting relationship habits.
Interventions:	Parenting education will be provided to the guardian. Therapist will teach conflict-resolution skills to the family.
Modalities:	Family therapy two times per month for a total of three hours.
Target date:	Nine weeks.

Client #4: Chauncey (age four)

According to Chauncey's case manager and mother, Chauncey exhibits persistent defiance, impulsivity, and aggression (verbal and physical) on a daily basis. He is also destructive in the home environment and exhibits disregard for safety or any interventions by adults around him. He often requires physical restraint to maintain safety. Chauncey's mother is a single parent who reports feeling exhausted and overwhelmed by her child's behaviors. The mother admits to being inconsistent with her parenting methods.

Treatment Plan

Name: Chauncey
Therapist: Mike Fulkerson, LPCC, CT/RTC
Strengths: Active, strong-willed, independent, and inquisitive
Needs: Acceptance of limits
Abilities: Intelligent
Preferences: Playing with toys and less structured environments
Input from client: Chauncey's mother is asking for help in learning to manage her child's behavior

Problem #1:	Mood disorder, NOS (Not Otherwise Specified)
Targeted behaviors:	Physical aggression toward others and himself, including head-banging, biting, hitting, kicking, and AWOL risk.
Baseline:	Multiple hospitalizations, including two within the past four months.
Goal #1:	Client will demonstrate stabilization of mood and aggressive behaviors as evidenced by ninety consecutive days without requiring hospitalization.
Objective #1:	Client will manage his emotions successfully during a thirty-day period free of safety crisis-management holds.
Objective #2:	While in the presence of his therapist, client will demonstrate at least three newly acquired skills of managing his emotions.
Modalities:	Individual therapy twice monthly.

Interventions:	Play therapy and relaxation training. Activate crisis safety plan.
Problem #2:	Oppositional defiant disorder
Target behaviors:	Uncooperativeness with others.
Baseline:	Client is currently hospitalized and transitioning to therapeutic foster care.
Goal #1:	Client will be reunited with his mother.
Objective #1:	Client will complete three task assignments given by therapist.
Objective #2:	Client will have a successful "trial exit" from therapeutic foster care measured by no required intervention from on-call therapeutic foster care staff.
Modalities:	Individual therapy twice monthly.
Interventions:	Play therapy
Problem #3:	Parent-child conflict
Targeted behaviors:	Chauncey shows disregard for limits set by parent.
Baseline:	The mother reports wanting more education and confidence to manage Chauncey's challenging behavior on a daily basis due to Chauncey's unwillingness to accept limits as well as instant desire for gratification. Chauncey's mother scored a 15 on the choice theory parenting survey.
Goal #1:	Chauncey's mother will improve her choice theory parenting survey score by least 10 percentage points.
Objective #1:	Chauncey's mother will read one book applying the principles of choice theory to parenting.
Objective #2:	Chauncey's mother will state that she feels more confident and prepared to manage Chauncey's behavior when he returns home.
Modalities:	Family therapy twice monthly.
Interventions:	Reality therapy, parenting psychoeducation.

Discharge Plan

Behavioral indicators that child/family is ready for discharge: Client will be reunified with mother once he demonstrates stability of mood and behaviors as indicated by a period of ninety consecutive days without requiring hospitalization.

Goal for level of care/support for the child/family at discharge: To return to the biological family, home of his mother, and follow up with impact plus services and therapeutic child support services.

Crisis Action Plan

Symptoms/behaviors that indicate a crisis: Defiance, verbal and physical aggression.

Strategies to Manage Crises

    #1: Provide empathic statements and encourage cooperation.

    #2: Set firm limits and focus Chauncey on current behavior.

    #3: Encourage Chauncey to make self-evaluation of choices.

    #4: Assist Chauncey in making a plan to do better.

    #5: Allow natural consequences except in cases where safety is in question.

    #6: Consult with on-call staff or therapist regarding treatment interventions.

Client #5: Jerry (Age 56)

Jerry is a fifty-six-year-old male who has been dealing with addiction to alcohol for many years. According to Jerry, his addiction to alcohol destroyed his career, marriage, and his relationships with his children, who no longer have contact with him. For the past several years, Jerry has been in and out of rehab treatment programs and homeless shelters. With the exception of living in a controlled setting, Jerry has been unable to maintain sobriety for longer than a period of two or three months. He has just completed another twenty-eight-day inpatient program and is continuing treatment on an outpatient basis.

Treatment Plan

Name: Jerry
Therapist: Mike Fulkerson, LPCC, CT/RTC
Strengths: Personable, social, and intelligent
Needs: To remain sober when living outside a controlled setting (rehab, shelters, etc.)
Abilities: Excellent "handy man" skills and articulate in speech
Preferences: He identifies himself as having a preference for being around others. Jerry says he likes "making others happy."
Input from client: Client states "I want to get clean and sober so I can get my life back."

Problem #1:	Substance use disorder
Targeted behaviors:	The inability to remain sober outside a controlled setting.
Baseline:	For the past several years, Jerry has been unable to remain sober for longer than two or three months outside a controlled setting.
Goal:	Jerry will maintain sobriety for at least six months outside a controlled setting.
Objective #1:	Jerry will complete a cost/benefit analysis of three desired changes he wants to make in his life.
Objective #2:	Jerry will attend ninety AA meetings in ninety days.
Objective #3:	Jerry will identify the function(s) his substance use has been serving in terms of meeting his needs for love/belonging, power, freedom, and fun.
Objective #4:	Jerry will develop a written strategy to replace his substance-abuse behaviors by listing alternative pathways to fulfill each of his unmet needs.
Objective #5:	Jerry will develop a written relapse-prevention plan that will include a list of warning signs, effective coping skills, and a contact list of people who can help him.

Interventions: Providing Jerry with information regarding the use of choice theory and reality therapy as a self-help method in addition to other cognitive-behavioral techniques, such as cognitive restricting, guided imagery, and reframing. A cost/benefit analysis will be used to assess Jerry's desire to change as well as his commitment to maintaining sobriety.

Modalities: Individual therapy for one hour per week.

Chapter 7: Comparing Treatment Planning from a Reality Therapy Perspective to Other Psychotherapy Models

7. Comparing Treatment Planning from a Reality Therapy Perspective to Other Therapy Models

In classical psychoanalysis and traditional psychodynamic approaches, the analyst is the expert on the client's experience as well as treatment planning. The interest is limited to what is going on within the individual client. The interpretation of the analyst is what is valid. Little attention is paid to external environment or stimuli or the organism's response to stimuli.

With behavior modification, the behaviorist is the expert and is only interested in the stimuli and the response but has no interest in the experience of the client. The role of the behavioral therapist is to mold the client's behavior through the use of reinforcement. Treatment planning decisions are made by the behaviorist.

The cognitive-behavioral therapist is interested in the stimuli, the client's responses, and the client's cognitive functioning. Although treatment goals are developed collaboratively with the client, the cognitive-behavioral therapist is still viewed as the expert. More recently, cognitive-behavioral therapists have become more interested in what is happening to the client emotionally as well as cognitively.

Humanistic/existential therapies take into account the client's own phenomenological perspective of the environment and the responses to outside stimuli. Both the therapist and the client are considered experts of their own phenomenological worlds. These therapies tend to view clients as having the ability to find solutions to their own problems so that humanistic/existential therapists may have a less active role in the client's treatment planning.

Postmodern or constructivist models, such as solution-focused therapy and narrative therapy, are based on the idea that human beings create their own personal view of the world. These approaches emphasize the idea of clients as experts of their own lives. Many of the newer approaches to psychotherapy are more symptom-focused and are often comprised of specific interventions designed to address specific diagnoses. In the opinion of this author, although some of the postmodern approaches have evidence to support their effectiveness, these evidenced-based methods are much more likely to be enhanced if the practicing clinician has a solid theoretical model as a foundation for the evidenced-based intervention. Occasionally, a clinician can become so focused on treating symptoms that more global issues may be missed. This problem could be analogous to a patient with a broken leg being treated only for a sore throat.

In my opinion, a reality therapy perspective to treatment planning takes a more comprehensive approach. Like the cognitive-behaviorist, the reality therapist is interested in stimuli and all environmental conditions that might impact the perception of the client, including culture, family, religion, economics, etc. The choice theory perspective sees activity, cognition, feelings, and physiological symptoms as interrelated but occurring in a less sequential process than other cognitive-behavioral approaches. Unlike other cognitive-behavioral therapists, the reality therapist does not see the client's thinking as being the primary issue. Instead, the reality therapist views the cognitions as a part of the total behavior, which is designed to reduce perceptual differences between what the client wants and what the client perceives he/she is getting from the external world. The reality therapist also recognizes that human beings have internal needs, especially the need for love/belonging. Thus, more emphasis is given to the importance of relationships than with most other cognitive-behavioral therapies. The perceptual differences between the quality world and the perceived world would be how a reality therapist would define a client's problem.

Similar to humanistic/existential approaches, reality therapists have an interest in how clients perceive the world around them as well as how they choose to respond to environmental stimuli. Clients are seen as "the experts" of their own perceptions and quality world pictures as well as treatment goals. Plus, there is an emphasis on the importance of relationships, which is reminiscent of Carl Rogers's work. Although clients are viewed as the experts of their own treatment goals, the reality therapist has the freedom to assume a more directive role when clients lack the necessary information and skills to find solutions to their problems. This reality therapy perspective provides a nice balance between giving clients the autonomy of being experts of their own lives while providing them with the necessary information to cope with their unsatisfied quality world pictures.

Earlier in my career, I can remember really being attracted to person-centered therapy. Thinking that the person-centered counseling style might be best suited for me, I read *A Way of Being* by Carl Rogers. The person-centered perspective about how to engage with clients resonated with me. Although I believed this approach was effective with some clients, the majority of my clients seemed to need more than just a trusting relationship.

Reality therapy was able to fill in the gaps by providing a comprehensive, holistic approach that when practiced most effectively includes some of the best aspects of the other schools of psychotherapy. With an emphasis on relationships and self-evaluation, reality therapy has a clearly defined theory to support it which make it unique to the field of psychotherapy Dr. William Glasser has developed a method of helping people that can be easily integrated into other methods of psychotherapy. In my opinion, the flexibility and adaptability of reality therapy are two of the approach's greatest assets.

Appendix

Expectations of TCS/Intensive In-Home Services

What We Will Do for You
1. Help you identify your goals for the program.
2. Help you determine what is effective and ineffective in reaching these goals.
3. Provide information regarding alternative strategies to reach your goals.
4. Suspend judgment regarding your past efforts to achieve your goals.
5. Maintain confidentiality with the exception of the information that is necessary to ensure someone's safety.
6. Provide a need-fulfilling atmosphere to encourage family enrichment.

What We Will Not Do for You
1. Tell you how to be a parent or how to live your life.
2. Give you a quick-fix solution. Things often get worse before they get better.
3. Take credit for your successes or failures.
4. Be providers or receivers of food, rewards, transportation, or money.
5. Be a babysitter or part of a companionship program.
6. Have our services used as a reward or punishment.
7. Communicate through e-mail, texting, or social media.

What You Will Be Expected to Do
1. Keep appointments and be punctual. Two unexcused absences could result in being placed back on a waiting list for services.
2. *Dedicate as much as three hours per week to our sessions.
3. Work hard.
4. Remain focused on family treatment goals and objectives.

What You Will Not Be Expected to Do
1. Make a long-term commitment to our program.
2. Tolerate our staff not honoring their commitments.
3. Provide staff with gifts, money, gift cards, etc. (Accepting gifts is a violation of agency policy and professional ethical codes.)

*Intensive in-home services only.
Your signature below indicates that you understand and are in agreement with the expectations listed above.

_____

(Signature) Date   (Witness)   Date

Basic Needs Assessment for Child/Youth

Baseline date:
Midtreatment date:
Closure date:

Please use a 0–10 scale (with 0 being the lowest and 10 being the highest) to answer the following questions.

1. How physically healthy are you?

2. How well do you get along with the important people in your life?

3. How well do you like yourself?

4. How much control do you feel you have over your life?

5. How much fun/enjoyment are you having in your life?

Name of child:

Staff:

Basic Needs Assessment by Parent(s) of Child/Youth

Baseline date:

Midtreatment date:

Closure date:

Please use the following 0–10 scale (with 0 being the lowest and 10 being the highest) to answer the following questions.

1. How physically healthy is your child?

2. How well does your child get along with others?

3. Rate your child's self-esteem.

4. How much self-control does your child possess?

5. How much does your child seem to enjoy life?

Name of child:

Staff:

THE REALITY THERAPY SANDWICH

SELF-EVALUATION

ACTION PLANNING (SPECIFIC, SIMPLE, IMMEDIATE, INDEPENDENT, & START PLAN)

ASSESSING LOCUS OF CONTROL

EXPLORING CURRENT BEHAVIORS (ACTIONS, THOUGHTS, FEELINGS & PHYSIOLOGY)

OBTAINING A COMMITMENT

EXPLORING QUALITY WORLD PICTURES

RELATIONSHIPS
SEVEN CARING HABITS:
1. SUPPORTING   5. TRUSTING
2. ENCOURAGING   6. RESPECTING
3. LISTENING   7. NEGOTIATING
4. ACCEPTING

ADAPTED FROM THE WORKS OF DR WILLIAM GLASSER

FULKERSON/HOLCOMB
2008

Brief Note about the Author

Michael Fulkerson is a licensed professional clinical counselor employed at River Valley Behavioral Health based in Owensboro, Kentucky. He serves as the program manager of therapeutic child support services. Mr. Fulkerson is also a faculty member of William Glasser International. His past work experiences have included inpatient therapy, domestic violence and substance abuse counseling, therapeutic foster care, and adjunct faculty status at Lindsey Wilson College.

Bibliography

———. *Choice Theory Manager.* New York: Harper Perennial, 1994.

Glasser, W. *Choice Theory.* New York, NY: Harper Collins, 1998.

———. *Defining Mental Health as a Public Health Issue.* Chatsworth, CA: The William Glasser Institute, 2005.

———. *Take Charge of Your Life.* Bloomington, IN: iUniverse, 2011.

Glasser, W., and Glasser, C. *Getting Together and Staying Together.* New York, NY: Harper Collins, 2000.

Jacobs, E. *Impact Therapy.* Lutz, FL: Psychological Assessment Resources, Inc., 1994.

Rogers, C. *A Way of Being.* Boston: Houghton Mifflin, 1980.

Wubbolding, R. *Reality Therapy for the 21st Century.* Philadelphia, PA: Brunner Routledge, 2000.

———. *Reality Therapy: Theories of Psychotherapy Series.* Washington, DC: American Psychological Association, 2011.